Emotionally Connected

Tracy Benson

BookLeaf Publishing

India | USA | UK

Presentation by *BookLeaf Publishing*

Web: www.bookleafpub.com

E-mail: info@bookleafpub.com

ISBN: 9789360944261

First edition 2024

This book is dedicated to my son Takari. Since becoming a mom I have a whole new sense of living life and what it means. My hope is that over time as you grow to read and understand each one of these poems it will give you a greater sense of your mother's journey in life before you and how now you are experiencing the best versions of me without filters.

ACKNOWLEDGEMENT

I would like to express my gratitude to all those who have supported and inspired me throughout my journey. To my son, Takari, you have become my biggest inspiration since the day you were born. The love you give me is unmatched. I'm blessed to have you. I love you buddy!

PREFACE

This collection of poems serves as an exploration of the vast spectrum of my emotions. You will find poems that dive into my depths of joy, love, hope, sadness and everything in between. Each poem is a collection of feelings that have shaped my experiences.

Poetry has always had a unique ability to capture my innermost thoughts and feelings in which I hope my words touch the hearts of readers across time. As you take this journey through these pages I hope you resonate with the emotions expressed within and that these poems serve you in your own personal way.

And a Piece of Me was Born

Even though the thought never crossed my
mind, you can never know where you will be,
who you will be with or what you will be doing
when it comes to time.
I was preparing without preparing and didn't
have a clue.
That through all the ups and downs, highs and
lows I was preparing for you.
Everything makes sense when I see your face.
Now that you are here all the things I thought I
did wrong no longer seem out of place.
You fill me with so much joy and make me feel
like the luckiest mom ever.
I swear, no matter what you face in life, good or
bad, we will always face everything together.

When am I enough

I didn't get a handbook on how to live life,
what to do, what not to say, if I was violated or
disrespected how do you determine when it's
enough to leave or maybe should I stay?
Do I deal with people lying to me, the broken
promises, the risk to gamble this special, rare
and sacred love or friendship that I so freely give
away. The selfish unloving actions.
What would be enough to stay, do I just continue
to hope for the best and move in an orderly
fashion
Why is it that people always want to see if the
other side of the grass is greener as if there could
be something better.
Why is it I can't find anyone that is only
concerned about our grass and just watering it
together.
The fake smiles, phony interests in my life were
all a bluff.
No matter what I do, show up, show out,
motivate, cater to everyone's needs, it seems to
never be enough.

Too late

I'm not perfect, tell me one person that is, I'll
wait.
Was I so blind by the lies, the phony eyes, the
fairy tale conversations that I didn't see the hate.
Yep hate, had to be, to do something so
thoughtless and cruel like this to me.
Me, the one that only motivates you and wants
you to be great, so mentally, emotionally and
physically challenged that you can't breathe
without me.
Can't lift your hand to scratch your head, I was
your rib, the soul in your body, but you had to
see.
You wanted to see anyway if the drug known as
myself was anywhere else.
Someone to make you weak to the touch.
Now things are different, I was the secret
ingredient. Don't be sad, don't be sorry; not
having that feeling is rough. That's gotta be
tough.

I don't want to hurt anymore

Is being happy too much to ask for.
Yes, we make our own decisions, I know, I get
it. But we don't know if it's the right one, you
know, the one that makes us sad, confused, used
and abused.
So again I ask, is being happy too much to ask
for.
I just want to smile all day, feel loved in every
possible way, hold another's hand, man I want
that to the core.
Someone authentic; these are my roots, that type
of love, that electric connection, those mirrored
reflections.
Everything in me tells me I deserve it. To be
happy, to honor and cherish, to be the greatest. I
know what I'm doing it for.
The companionship, the touches, the shared
plates and dinner dates.
I just don't want to hurt anymore.

The one I fell in love with

I've always been a hopeless romantic, so yea, I
believe in true love. That real, special, deep I'll
never hurt you type of love.
That no matter what, you can't do wrong in my
eyes, I'll always cheer for you the loudest type of
love.
Now did I ever think I would find it. Well, I sure
did. A love that I knew was all mine..
I had a love that was sacred, and real that gave
me chills down my spine..

The best things are sometimes unexpected.
I carried this love with me, I grew and nurtured
this love. Over time this love grew stronger. This
love that I can't dare to pull away.
This love is a part of me, it needs me here, I am
this love's home, I don't have to beg it to stay.
When I saw the face of this love there's no way I
have felt this love before.
This love feels amazing, it feels real and safe, it
gives me chills I can't ignore.
I fell in love with this love before a second. I'll
carry it through everything.
The best love I can ever have, our journey is
never done.

Change

I've heard over time people can change, no one
stays the same, we all grow right.
Wrong, not everyone can be a better person and
I know that sounds harsh to say, but it's true.
When people do decide to mature and grow does
it matter if it's for a good reason, shouldn't you
want to change for you.
You want to be a good person.
You want to do the right things.
Sometimes the way we get older and how we
start to think can be a shock to ourselves, what
really does growth mean.
I think we all have our own thoughts and
processes unique to them, no one's exactly the
same.
But if you can go through life without any
growth and you don't want to do right by people
or yourself, you are only to blame.

My Son

You are the reason I breathe life into my body these days.

There are a million things I can do to express my love for you and I promise to do it in all ways.

You will know you are protected and that I'll protect you the best way I can with everything in me.

I promise to always support you, love you and guide you forever in life, you will see.

I didn't understand true love before I met you.

I accepted what was given to me but you have given me the understanding of my worth and that's the truth.

I'll only expect you to be great in whatever purpose you choose for your life.

I want so much happiness in your world. I want you to love what you do, make good decisions and find a beautiful, caring, nurturing and loving wife.

Someone I know that will care for you very closely to how I do but no one could love you more, it's just not possible to me.

I'll be giving you the best version of me everyday and I'll never let you down as you progress and grow through life, you will see.

The best part of me was born Nov 26th, my life changed that day. God blessed me with my son. I don't care about a lottery ticket, a new car or anything else, just having you born validates to me that I've won.

Men make me laugh

Man I'll tell you, if I had a penny for every man
that claimed he was the best, was loyal, was
faithful and that he was ready for
companionship, do you know I would be rich.
I'll never understand the need to lie, why just say
you are not ready, say you like being single,
ready to mingle, then you disrespect me, take
my love for granted then when I'm fed up, it's all
on me.
What's the point, waste my time, break your
promises, stand me up on our dates.
I wish as a little girl, yes even that small
someone started warning me that men aren't that
great.
Tell me I have to have thick skin, that I have to
accept men aren't made up of fairies and gods.
That sometimes we won't always get along, we
won't be each other's favorite person, sometimes
we will be at odds.
Tell me they think they are slick, they can plot,
scheme and get away with some things.
Crazy thing is you can have a man do all this
wrong to you and have the nerve to still get on
one knee with a ring.
That's just so funny to me.

Hot then cold, starts clean but after you have
marinated the dirt is exposed. Puts me in the
mind of when we take baths.
Man, men are a piece of work, they will never
have a clue. That's why I say men make me
laugh.

Does the pain go away

No matter how long I cry or how red my eyes
get, I can't get this pain to go away.
I just want to stop hurting, I want to smile again,
this pain I feel is making me sad.
Why me, all I've tried to do was be a good
person, treat people how I like to be treated, yes
I do believe in all of that.
Man I used to be such a happy person before
when can I get that back.
I'm seeking it, I miss her, she was the best.
I won't let this pain that's inflicted on me kill
that woman. It's not worth the stress.

My happy face prince

I could have only imagined that I would have the
most beautiful baby in the world.
So silly, so sweet, so already quick on his feet,
strong heartbeat, I'm a lucky girl.
Feeling blessed is not enough. I'm overjoyed,
grateful, special, yea all that other stuff.
I already poured my heart, soul, my young and
old into my precious part of me.
I show him unconditional love, I cater to every
cry, never shall I watch tears run down your
eyes, that's how it should be.
Days and weeks and months and years I get to
watch you grow. How much I love you, I'll show
you in every breath that I take so that you know.
You are my everything, you are my heartbeat,
my purpose, you ignite the soul in me.
My baby boy, my prince, my joy, my happy
face, little man, you are me.

Today is a better day

Yesterday was rough, crying all day, being sad about bad decisions that are not mine, man that's tough.
That trust word is real, someone violates you, disrespects you, you feel undervalued, I lost my trust because of how you made me feel.
I love you everyday, want to love you in every way tell me how things get better.

Just do the right thing by me, I promise I won't make it hard. The last thing I want is to think about us being apart,
How you make me feel safe, are loyal, faithful and I just praise you like you are a star.
I know you love me too because when we argue that love is expressed right through you.
You love me being in your life, you want me to be your wife, don't waste our time, I am all you need, that's what I heard you say.
I'm always happy now, never second guessing myself, doesn't mean it can't be a better day.

Maybe I'm ok, maybe I'm not

Yep, bad days seem to come a dime a dozen
these days.
But I try to channel my energy to move past
these feelings in those ways.
The ways that always have me staring in the
mirror with big red puffy eyes from tears taking
over my face.
I don't want anyone to know I'm sad, I should be
strong, need to know nothing's wrong,
everything's in place.
In place, what does that mean anyway, is it
home, I seem to always think about what I need
to do almost every other day.
But I'm ok, at least I have to be right.
I have so many things I need to be strong for,
suck it up Tracy, stand 10 toes down and fight.
But what am I fighting for anymore, bonds that
were broken, I feel like my love is always taken
for granted, it's just been a lot.
I try to believe better days will come and they
will, I'll forgive when necessary but don't think I
forgot, anyway, maybe I'm ok, then again,
maybe I'm not.

My Love

You lit a fire in me I had no clue I had, this
newfound strength in me.
You give me joy that I didn't know existed, all
these years I thought I was in love but no one
told me this love is how it should be.
You make me feel like the whole world could
stop, no movement, only us two in this world
called life.
I could stare at you all day but even everyday is
not enough, that won't even suffice.
When our eyes connect even now, still
depending on me you tell me, mom I got you.
You and me, I'll always have your back, promise
to never break your heart.
My beautiful son, this is the type of connection
we have, giving and showing me unconditional
love from the start.
One thing is for certain, and I promise you this,
every second you grow, your first words, your
ever changing personality until it settles, I will
never miss.
You show me so much love, give me so much
grace and you make me feel like I'm enough,
son, I've always wanted this.

I'm feeling great

Is it possible to process through your emotions
and still be able to say I'm good.
It's crazy how we always say what we would or
wouldn't do cause I didn't make any of those
decisions like I should.
It's easy to give advice and sound like a pro
when you do it, but why can't we take our own.
So many different outcomes if I could have seen
the future if I'd known.
Everyday I'm pushing through all these
important decisions that I have to make.
But I'm on the road to better, I know because
today I'm actually feeling great.

Closed for repair

They say they are damaged, broken, angry and
all these things. I say I'm just closed for repairs.
You want me to just move on, start over and
forget my heart was broken when the hurt is still
there.
I'm not a robot or light switch, my emotions
can't immediately be turned off at the flick of a
wrist.
I still cry at night, still ask myself those
clarifying questions, why would someone who
says they love me do me like this.
You don't want to be tied down, no commitment,
come and go as you please, then why not leave
me be.
I still may think about you, reminisce cause
some feelings are still there.
But no, not damaged, not broken, not angry, just
closed for repair.

Don't give up, it gets better

Happy, sad, angry, mad, feeling all these
different emotions, I know it's draining but don't
give up, it gets better.
Life is so much more than failed relationships,
bad partners and constant heartbreak.
It's about more than ignoring your wants and
needs and undergoing the ups and downs of so
much stress, this out of controlness you don't
have to take.
Raise your head, straighten your shoulders, walk
like you can't be defeated.
Take all the time to motivate your mind and feel
powerful again, trust me you need it.
Everyday is a new day, take control of your life,
don't let anyone take your joy ever.
Raise your head, straighten your shoulders,
walk like you can't be defeated.
Don't give up, it gets better.

Emotions

I feel all these emotions on different days of the
week.
I don't fight my emotions anymore; they are a
part of me.
When I love, I love hard and my feelings get all
wired up, no more feelings bottled up.
You know when I'm sad, happy, maybe nothing
or maybe in between.
But I won't hide it.
I won't be ashamed, I won't change I want these
emotions to be appreciated, love me
more because of it.
I embrace my ability to tap into all my
vibrations, we are beautiful.
I am BEAUTIFUL!

My Girls

My girls, my girls, my homies, my happy, no
matter what they show up whenever,
however, front and center.
They show up and love me, encourage me,
remind me that I'm always a winner.
My girls, we be booked and busy with life,
families, hobbies but when I call, here they
come.
Good vibes, good energy, that's what my girls
bring me. Always positive, channeling all
the good, they are showing out for me.

To say I'm lucky is an understatement, I would
give these girls the world. I am so
grateful and so blessed to call them my girls.

When I lost you

The day I lost you, I lost my heartbeat, my need
to speak, I'm no longer the strong black
woman, I am now weak.
Weak to the core, fragile bones and dusty veins,
who knew hurt could hurt this bad.
You were everything to me, the main reason I
want to grow up and be great, to make sure
You are proud.
Who knew it doesn't take noise to be heard, that
silence can be so loud.
Mama I miss you, your touch, your smile, your
smell. Not a day goes by that I don't wish
you were still here. There's forever a hole in my
heart and at times the feeling of what
may be hell.

It's always so dark, so cold and now so lonely,
and listen to this, I made you a grandma.
He will know you for sure, I show him pictures
and tell him stories about you everyday.
I will never forget you, not celebrate you, not
remember you, there will never be a day.

9 789360 944261